Inward Outward Upward

Art Sathoff

Inward Outward Upward

Art Sathoff

Published by 1st World Publishing
P.O. Box 2211, Fairfield, Iowa 52556
tel: 641-209-5000 • fax: 866-440-5234
web: www.1stworldpublishing.com

First Edition

LCCN: 2016900615

ISBN: 978-1-4218-3747-5

Acknowledgements

I would like to thank my parents, Craig and Mary Sathoff, for first teaching me what God's love is about. They are both with God now themselves. Thank you also to the spiritual leaders I have known through the years, especially Harlan "Frosty" Van Voorst, who encouraged my spiritual growth a great deal. Finally, thank you to my immediate family: my loving wife Cindy, who helped put my life on a different path, and our sons Jordan and Trey, who also know the joy of a personal relationship with our Creator.

Introduction

I was at an annual assembly of the Christian Church (Disciples of Christ) years ago, and the theme was "Inward, Outward, Upward." At the time that denomination was doing some soul searching and restructuring as a result of economic difficulties, and the theme provided an entry point for examining the inner workings of the church, the church's relationships with those outside the church and denomination, and with our Father above.

The day I began this book, years after the church assembly, I referred to the same theme to describe efforts to bring community leaders representing different groups and institutions together. These leaders each have to focus inward to run their organizations effectively, but they can't afford not to have an outward focus on other organizations, and they also focus upward as they seek to craft stronger organizations for community progress and the good of their citizens.

I am a big believer in reflection and introspection. I have referred to the inscription above the Oracle at Delphi in ancient Greece before: "Know Thyself." I believe we have to be at peace with ourselves and take care of the *inward* before we can be much good to others, but the longer I live, the more I realize that we really need to cultivate the *outward*, too. Granted, my chosen professions of teacher, coach, school administrator, and pastor are much more relationship-driven than some other occupations. Still, I believe that happy and productive people understand the power of relationships and have mastered the *outward*. For me, personally, the inward and outward have been enhanced tremendously by a focus on the *upward*. My Christian faith has brought about positive changes in my life, benefiting both the inward and outward. I'm sure there are other higher causes that provide *upward* benefits for people, too.

This book is going to be an exploration of the inward, outward, and upward. It is organized into three parts, containing six exhortations each. Each of the six exhortations is a chapter relating a theme that runs inward, outward, and upward through all three parts of the book. At the risk of confusing the reader, I'll share that I wrote Chapter 1 in each section before going on to Chapter 2 and so on. If you don't mind turning back and forth between inward, outward, and upward, you can read it in the order I wrote it. Otherwise, you can read it section by section.

The best thing that could happen with this book is that someone would read it and benefit from it. If you find the book helpful or want to discuss the book, please feel free to email me at sathofar@gmail.com Enjoy!

Contents

Section 1 – Inward

Section 2 – Outward

Section 3 – Upward

Section 1 — Inward

Chapter 1
Be Honest With Yourself

"If you do not tell the truth about yourself you cannot tell it about other people."

—Virginia Woolf

I am saddened to even be writing the exhortation, "Be honest with yourself." Are people really so self-deluding that they have to be encouraged to be honest with themselves? Unfortunately, the answer is a resounding, "Yes!"

There are innumerable games we play with ourselves, mental gymnastics to avoid being honest with ourselves. We have become skilled rationalizers. We are excuse makers extraordinaire. People cry, "That's not me!" when they do stupid, immoral, or hurtful things. "It was a momentary lapse of judgment," or "I'm just overwhelmed right now." You know the drill. Rather than acknowledge our thoughtlessness, disinterest, or selfishness, we try to put a bow on this behavior, pretty it up, and excuse it. A couple of colloquial truisms come to mind: "You can put lipstick on a pig, but it's still a pig," and "You can't make a silk purse out of a sow's ear." These porcine examples could be coming to mind because my weight is near an all-time high. I'm being honest with myself.

An important first step in being honest with yourself is to recognize your blind spots and your selfish motives. Humanists haven't made this easy to do through the ages because their fundamental belief is in the essential goodness of human nature. This leaves them explaining away why people do all of the rotten things they do. I choose to believe in what some call the *depravity of man* because I have a biblical worldview. I believe that human nature is sinful, and I believe there is evil in the world. That doesn't mean I don't look for good in people or that I am a misanthrope who hates humanity. On the contrary, I believe we all have a spark of the divine since we were created in God's image. We just need to start with the fundamental understanding that "all sin and fall short of the glory of God" (Romans 3:23). Once we confess that, we can be honest, and we can quit trying to rationalize sinful behavior.

I have gotten to the point that I am pretty honest with myself. I'm comfortable praying the prayer of the tax collector: "Lord, have mercy on me, a sinner" (Luke 18:13). I don't have to live with the dissonance of wanting to think of myself one way and acting and speaking another way. I strive to be a genuine person and "walk the talk," but I acknowledge my shortcomings. I take the Pharisees, whom Jesus was so critical of for being hypocritical, (Matthew 23:1-3, Luke 11:37-44) as a cautionary tale.

I have to admit that I was pretty good at kidding myself

for a lot of years. I thought of myself as a good Christian and a good person, but my actions often didn't bear that out. John could have been writing about me when he penned, "Whoever says, 'I know him,' but does not keep his commandments is a liar, and the truth is not in him, but whoever keeps his word, in him truly the love of God is perfected. By this we may know that we are in him: whoever says he abides in him ought to walk in the same way on which he walked" (1 John 2:4-6). I probably portrayed myself as pretty confident (okay, cocky), but I didn't feel good about myself. And if you don't feel good about yourself, you're not going to feel very good about others. Fortunately, I learned how to deal with disappointments in life, I realized I wasn't a very happy person, and I married a great woman. My faith became stronger and began to guide my life. I began to live for my family and faith as well as for myself. I began to do a better job of owning my imperfections and became more comfortable in my own skin.

I am under no illusions that I have "arrived" and have everything all figured out. I know myself pretty well, though, and I'm honest with myself. I understand my tendencies, and I am generally a self-disciplined person. I know I'm a smart aleck and a wise-cracker, and there still are probably times I should keep my mouth shut when I don't. I'm hyper-competitive, but I have learned how to deal with defeat and I'm not as bad a sport as I used to be. I'm not always demonstrative, but I'm getting better at letting people know I care. I'm also learning to "let go and let God" more; and while I still like things to go according to <u>my</u> plan, I've gotten pretty good at not worrying about what I can't control. I am still too much "of this world" in comparison to what a strong Christian should be. While I happily give of my time and money, I don't give enough. I'm sometimes selfish. I want to take credit for the good things in my life. I do a poor job of seeing the world and other people through God's eyes. I am judgmental.

God still loves me, though, and He's not finished with me yet. I know myself well enough and am honest enough with myself to catch myself and do mid-course corrections most of the time I am being a jerk or going too far. I have God's Word to convict me, the Spirit to encourage me, and accountability partners like my awesome wife to keep it real.

Think about it: what's getting in the way of your being honest with yourself?

1. Do you feel pressure to be something you're not?
2. Are you unclear about what your core values are?
3. Is there dissonance between what you say you believe and what your actions show?
4. If you were on trial for being a good spouse, a good parent, a good friend, a good employee, or a good Christian, would there be enough evidence to convict you?
5. Have you ever written down what is important to you? If not, think about writing a credo, or statement of belief.
6. Would your spouse, friends, or co-workers describe you the same way you describe yourself?

Chapter 2
Push Yourself

"Push yourself again and again. Don't give an inch until the final buzzer sounds."

—Larry Bird

I have a tough time understanding complacency. Why wouldn't people want to be their best? Why can't some people allow themselves (or their kids) to struggle a little bit, understanding that's how growth occurs? In coaching parlance this is "getting out of your comfort zone." I wish I had a dollar for every time I heard that important phrase uttered at Snow Valley Basketball School the years I worked there. I have a growth mindset and enjoy seeing personal growth more than just about anything else (Full disclosure moment in honor of Section 1, Chapter 1: my golf game has not improved much through the years, and I have not enrolled in any technical classes to address my mechanical shortcomings).

I grew up in a family that valued hard work and achievement, and I aspired to do the things my older brother did. This is how I learned to push myself. I have an inward drive to be successful although my definition of success has changed some through the years. I believe actions speak louder than words. Albert Schweitzer said it more eloquently: "I cannot hear your words because your actions speak so loudly." Wouldn't it be great if the world were full of self-motivated self-starters? How different would the world be if people didn't become stagnant and set in their ways?

It is probably important to consider the motivation behind this exhortation to "push yourself," too. I am not advocating for people to be driven and focused on one thing to the exclusion of other important things. For example, I am willing to bet that not many Division I athletic coaches need to be told to push themselves when it comes to work. The same thing is probably true of Fortune 500 CEOs. Many of them have probably pushed themselves to the detriment of their marriages or health. I also am not saying that we should never slow down and enjoy life or experience contentment. What I am suggesting is somewhat paradoxical: learning to be content in any and every situation like the Apostle Paul (Philippians 4:11-12) while pressing on toward the goal to win the prize, also like the Apostle Paul (Philippians 3:14).

I really am not comfortable prescribing to people specifically how they ought to live their lives (although all of my books share things that work for me). I am confident in saying that God expects us to grow and mature. The Bible chronicles Jesus' growth, telling us, "Jesus grew in wisdom and in stature and in favor with God and all the people"

(Luke 2:52). If the perfect Son of God grew, shouldn't we be expected to? Think of all of the farming/growth examples Jesus used in parables. Clearly there is an expectation of growth, and that doesn't happen without pushing yourself. I, personally, do not want to be like the unproductive fig tree that Jesus cursed and withered (Luke 13:6-9).

If we follow the first *inward* exhortation of being honest with ourselves, then that reflection suggests ways to push ourselves, or areas in which we need to grow. We also need to be coachable. Whether it's the wisdom of the Bible or the less perfect guidance from a boss, significant other, or friend, our high expectations can be informed by feedback from others. In education we constantly stress feedback and data. We attempt to set realistic goals that flow from a knowledge base we have constructed. These goals give realistic direction to the efforts to push ourselves. I need to understand that pushing myself will not make me a PGA golfer. It quite likely will make me a better Christian or husband or superintendent.

Push yourself to be your best. This is a very important *inward* exhortation. When I was a principal, I used to tell students that the more self-disciplined they were, the less anyone would have to impose discipline on them from the outside. This same thing is true for adults. If we are always pushing ourselves to be better Christians, better spouses, better parents, better employees, etc. our lives will undoubtedly be more satisfying and rewarding.

Chapter 3
Forgive Yourself

"Love yourself—accept yourself—forgive yourself—and be good to yourself, because without you the rest of us are without a source of many wonderful things."

—Leo F. Buscaglia

Self-loathing is a powerful thing. Sometimes people get trapped in a vicious cycle of sin and guilt and self-loathing. Guilt over our sin makes us feel worthless and unlovable. Someone who is feeling worthless and unlovable is more likely to sin further. Something has to intervene to break this toxic cycle, or lives will be destroyed.

Maybe you haven't committed such a horrible sin that you were left feeling worthless and unlovable. Maybe there's just some little thing about yourself that you can't get past. Maybe you can't resist gossiping, or maybe you view everybody you meet with a critical eye rather than a loving one. Chances are that the shortcomings you are so quick to notice in others are alive and well in you, preventing you from loving yourself so that you can love others (and thus the *inward* impacts the *outward*).

We can be our own worst critics sometimes. We hear that little voice of doubt telling us we aren't good enough, smart enough, or successful enough. We fall into comparison traps and end up feeling inferior. Let me ask you this: "Do you think you know more about yourself than the God who created you?" Was God wrong when He decided the sinful human race, including you and me, was worth forgiving and sending His Son to suffer and die for? You see, self-loathing is really an arrogant state of mind. It says that you know better than God what your worth is. Don't forget the natural order of things: "We love because God first loved us" (1 John 4:19). We can forgive ourselves and others because God has already forgiven us and "washed us white as snow," as the great old song "Jesus Paid it All" says.

Forgiving yourself doesn't mean having low standards or willfully committing the same sins over and over. Christ was incredibly forgiving and compassionate, but He still expected right living. He told the woman who faced death by stoning for adultery, "Neither do I condemn you" (John 8:11), but he followed that up with, "Go and sin no more," in that same verse. He went out of His way to give the Samaritan woman at the well Living Water, but He called her out on her immoral behavior (John 4). So you see, forgiving yourself is not a blank check for sinful behavior. Rather, it is acknowledgement that you are imperfect but striving to become more Christ-like.

I take the Lord's Prayer seriously, and I mean what I say when I recite it each night. "And forgive us our trespasses as we forgive those who trespass against us," is a powerful reminder. I have no right to expect to receive forgiveness if I don't extend forgiveness to others. If I'm struggling to forgive myself, that probably won't happen. As always, the *inward* and *outward* are linked. The only unforgivable sin I have seen discussed in the Bible is blaspheming against the Holy Spirit (Mark 3:28-29). "Judgment is mine," says the Lord (Romans 12:19). Our job is not to judge; it is to forgive. Rick Warren once wrote, "An unforgiving Christian is a contradiction in terms." If you are going to identify yourself as a Christian, you must forgive; and that starts with forgiving yourself.

Chapter 4
Be Bold

"Freedom lies in being bold."

—Robert Frost

Are you a bold and confident person? As a Christian, should you even aspire to be bold? After all, Jesus said, "The meek shall inherit the earth" (Matthew 5:5, KJV). We are the jewel of God's creation, and he didn't create us to be any less than our best, however. We can be meek in spirit and loving without being weak. Christ certainly was both compassionate and bold. Understanding that personalities differ and not everyone is wired to be brash, or extroverted, being bold in and for the Lord is still a biblical concept. Ephesians 3:13 says, "Because of Christ and our faith in him, we can now come boldly and confidently into God's presence" (LASB). Hebrews 4:16 exhorts, "So let us come boldly to the throne of our gracious God. There we will receive his mercy, and we will find grace to help us when we need it most" (LASB). The preceding verses provide the explanation of why we can do this: because we have a great High Priest in Jesus, who understands our weaknesses because he faced the same testings we did without sinning (Hebrews 4:14-15, LASB). If we can come boldly into God's presence, then clearly we ought to be able to boldly live our faith in our everyday lives.

When the Apostle Paul was advising his young pastor friend Timothy, he told him, "For God has not given us a spirit of fear and timidity, but of power, love, and self-discipline" (2 Timothy 1:7, LASB). We should be encouraged by this same advice. If we know the truth, understanding the Word is the source of real truth and that the Bible is God's written word and Jesus is "the word made flesh" (John 1:14), then we can live the way God intends us to. Paul says that is with power, love, and self-discipline. The marriage of these characteristics is awesome! We can be bold without harming others if we're living in love. With self-discipline we won't get carried away with our boldness. We won't behave recklessly and thoughtlessly.

What would our lives look like if we consistently lived with power, love, and self-discipline? Can you see how this is the perfect combination of characteristics? This is how Christ lived. Study His life and ministry: it's a study of power and compassion. And self-discipline? Imagine going to Jerusalem and the cross knowing the pain and anguish He would be facing. That's self-discipline and adherence to God's plan.

I pray that when we face moments of doubt and fear, we might draw power from the limitless reservoir of the Holy Spirit and go forward boldly. When we face situations when we are tempted to lash out, I pray that we can choose to respond with love instead, "finding grace to help us when we need it most" (Hebrews 4:16, LASB). When we are tempted and in danger of letting the world's values become our values, I pray that we can have self-discipline and not give in to sin. If we live our lives on earth this way, we will be prepared to "come boldly and confidently into God's presence" (Ephesians 3:13, LASB), and that is when it will <u>really</u> matter.

Chapter 5
"Be Young at Heart"

"Everyone is the age of their heart."

—Guatemalan Proverb

This entry is in the *inward* section, but being young at heart certainly impacts the *outward* and *upward*, too. Who doesn't love to be around a person who has the perpetual spark of youth at his/her core? Why do you think Jesus said we need to have the faith of a child (Matthew 18:3)? We all should be young at heart.

What does it mean to be young at heart exactly? Think joy. Think wonder. Think playfulness. Why are we so quick to brush these things aside, usually with a disapproving frown, in the adult world? Jesus had to rebuke His disciples: "Suffer the little children come unto me" (Matthew 19:14 KJB). He had to remind Martha that household chores would always be there, but He wouldn't be (Luke 10:41-42).

Mary, whom Martha was so annoyed with, actually had her priorities straight. A young heart is curious. It sees possibilities where a weary heart despairs. Cynicism and disappointment have not hardened a young heart.

Jesus referred to stubborn, unrepentant people as stiff-necked and hard-hearted. The Jews wandering in the wilderness and the self-righteous Jewish religious leaders both deserved those labels. Young hearts are teachable hearts. Jesus loved seekers with teachable hearts, like Nicodemus (John 3) and the Samaritan woman at the well (John 4). Young hearts know the world is a big, exciting place with much to teach us.

King David had a young heart. When he was a young man of twelve or so, he had the audacity to take on the giant who was bad-mouthing his God and terrorizing his people (1 Samuel 17). He didn't know that he shouldn't be able to defeat Goliath with a sling and a stone. Sometimes we are so busy telling kids, "No!" that I wonder how a young heart ever survives.

King David also shows the immaturity and egocentricity that a young heart can fall prey to. He lusts after Bathsheba and selfishly takes what he wants. He compounds his sin by plotting Uriah's death when the faithful soldier's nobility prevents David from covering up his adultery (2 Samuel 11). How can this adulterous murderer be described as "a man after God's own heart" (Acts 13:22, NIV)? Perhaps it was because he was teachable. God sends Nathan the prophet to David to help uncover his sin, and David confesses and repents (2 Samuel 12). David not only possessed a teachable heart but also a joyful heart. I love the description of David's approach to Jerusalem, known as the City of David: "Wearing a linen ephod, David was dancing before the Lord with all his might, while he and all Israel were bringing up the ark of the Lord with shouts and the sound of trumpets" (2 Samuel 6:14-15). What a great picture of a young heart that is, dancing with all his might before God!

I hope I never fully grow up. My family, friends, and people whom I work closely with probably feel that there is little danger of that. I am just so thankful for the blessings in my life, and I genuinely enjoy people. I see the humor in situations, and I choose to be positive and optimistic. Again, these are *inward* choices, but you'd better believe there are *outward* implications. People want to be around others who are positive and fun-loving. I believe God wants us to enjoy life and be young at heart.

Everyone is the age of their heart. I think I'm eternally pre-adolescent, and I'm fine with that.

Chapter 6
"In your Heart of Hearts, who are You?"

"Thou hast made us for thyself, O Lord, and our heart is restless until it finds its rest in thee."

—St. Augustine

"In your heart of hearts, who are you?" This is a dangerous question, one that becomes scarier as a person honestly reflects upon it. An honest self-assessment will expose the pettiness, the selfishness, and the sinfulness of the human heart. Calvinism refers to this condition as "the depravity of man." If you believe the Bible, humans are sinful by nature because of Original Sin, the Fall of Man in the Garden of Eden.

Even more dangerous than the realization that we are doomed and damned when left to our own devices is the belief of some people that human nature is basically good. The Age of Enlightenment, or Age of Reason, in the Seventeenth and Eighteenth Centuries emphasized human intellect and its ability to raise people up. The Romantic Era of the Nineteenth Century emphasized emotion and creativity much more but also idealized human nature. By the time Secular Humanism really came into its own in the 20th century, human nature was being considered separately from issues of faith. Many atheists today are descendants of these philosophies and consider themselves much too intelligent and enlightened to believe the superstitions and fairy tales of the Bible.

The Bible warned about a time when people would have "itching ears," just hearing what they wanted to hear (2 Timothy 4:3). 2 Peter 3:3 warns about "scoffers" coming in the last days, and that term perfectly describes today's atheists. During Jesus' day the Jewish religious leaders certainly were not humbling themselves as sinners. They were holding themselves up as paragons of virtue and patting themselves on the back for not being like the sinners (Luke 18:11). Jesus said they were all show. He compared them to cups that were clean on the outside but filthy on the inside (Matthew 23:25-26). Who wants to drink out of that?

The Holy Spirit had never touched those religious leaders' hearts, and many people today—even some identifying as Christians—have little to do with the Holy Spirit. Why is this? One of the key functions of the Spirit, besides encouraging and inspiring, is convicting us of sin. I know that I am a sinner. I recognize temptations that plague me. I know I can be a pretty rotten person if I am not living for Christ. I am not going to fall into the comparison trap of thinking I'm a good person because I go to church more often or give more generously than some other person. I am not deserving of eternal life just because I haven't killed someone or committed some other heinous crime. Sin is sin. I'm a sinner, and I can't save myself.

The Bible says we are slaves. We are either slaves to sin or slaves to righteousness (Romans 6:16). I have made my choice. I don't want to be a slave to sin. I would be lying if I said I aspired to be "in chains for Christ" (Philippians 1:13) like the Apostle Paul. I should welcome suffering if it advances God's kingdom. Maybe I will get to that point. I do trust that God will give me strength to handle trials in my life, and I think I understand what it means to be complete in weakness (2 Corinthians 12:9). In my heart of hearts, I believe God takes us in our brokenness and re-forms us into objects of beauty and utility like the potter does with the clay (Jeremiah 18:4).

Who am I in my heart of hearts? Without God I am rotten to the core, even if I convince myself I am a good person. With God I am dead to sin (Romans 6:11). I am a child of the light (1 Thessalonians 5:5). I am in this world but not of this world (John 17:16). I am salt and light (Matthew 5:13-16). I am co-heir of God's Kingdom with Christ (Romans 8:17). I am righteous, not because of my own doing but because of the suffering and sacrifice of Jesus Christ. In my heart of hearts, I am saved. And I am thankful.

Section 2 — Outward

Chapter 1
Be Authentic With Others

"No one man can, for any considerable time, wear one face to himself, and another to the multitude, without finally getting bewildered as to which is the true one."

—Nathaniel Hawthorne

I shared in Chapter 1 of Section 1 that I didn't think people could be real with others if they weren't honest with themselves. The good news is, once people have learned to be honest with themselves, having authentic relationships with others becomes easier and more enjoyable. Generally, people detect insincerity pretty well, and they are unforgiving if they think you are being disingenuous. On the other hand, people can be very forgiving if they think you are genuine and are being honest with them. If we are authentic with others, we can dispense with a lot of gamesmanship, and we can attain win-win relationships even with the inevitable occasional "agree to disagree."

My life as a school administrator the last fifteen years has made me place being genuine, or *transparent*, as everyone likes to say, at the top or near the top of the list of characteristics I prize and attempt to exhibit. People will not follow a leader they cannot trust. Cynics might try to convince you otherwise, but honesty still is the best policy. Of course, my parents raised me to be honest, and I haven't striven to be an honest school administrator just to prove that's not a contradiction in terms. Answering to many different people and groups with sometimes competing agendas gives school leaders and others the opportunity, or temptation, to say and do what is popular or expedient rather than what is right. Sometimes it is much easier not to have the hard conversation or to just choose to go with the flow. In my opinion good leaders consistently resist this temptation. People want their leaders to be real. Relationships with others consistently mirror how people feel about themselves. The *inward* and *outward* are in sync. Once again, *authentic* is the key word here. Don't think you can be like the politician who dons the flannel shirt when he goes out to the Midwestern farm on a campaign stop. That usually doesn't work for him either.

We have to overcome some things to be authentic with others. We have to realize we can't always make everyone happy, and that shouldn't be our primary goal anyway. Coaching taught me this before I was ever a school administrator. We also have to understand that being real doesn't mean being cruel. Many times as a school administrator I have had to call someone on inappropriate behavior. I tried to let people maintain their dignity when I had to do so. God knows that I have behaved inappropriately myself more than once. The Christian way of describing the approach I am advocating for is, "Hate the sin, but love the sinner."

We have all made mistakes, and we are all better off if we have been held accountable. However, I bet we all benefited more when the correction came with compassion and understanding. Galatians 6:1 suggests such an approach: "Brothers and sisters, if someone is caught in a sin, you who live by the Spirit should restore that person gently" (NIV). One of the most important things to overcome in order to be authentic with others is our pride. Too often leaders are prideful, like the Jewish religious leaders in the Bible were.

Jesus provides a great model of how to correct without condemnation (See John 8:3-11). He reminds the would-be executioners of the adulteress of their own sins when He says, "Very well, let he who is without sin cast the first stone." One by one the accusers slink away, beginning with the oldest (Ah, the wisdom of age!). Jesus doesn't condemn the accused either, but He does address her sinful behavior and expect a change: "Go and sin no more," He says.

The really difficult thing for some people to understand, I think, is the co-existence of accountability and forgiveness. Logically, there would be no need for forgiveness if there were no accountability. If there were no concept of sin or wrongdoing, there could be no concept of forgiveness either. Since there is sin, there is a need for forgiveness, and Christians pray, "Forgive us our sins as we forgive those who sin against us." Even when there is forgiveness, there are natural consequences of sin. If I caught an employee stealing from the school or drinking on the job, I could forgive him/her, but he/she would still become an ex-employee. Whether we are the one doing the correcting or the one being corrected, this accountability is just one way we are authentic with each other.

Chapter 2
High Expectations

"High expectations are the key to everything."

—Sam Walton

Is it egotistical to have high expectations for others? Does doing so somehow put us in a superior position? I would offer an emphatic, "No!" in reply as long as we first have high expectations for ourselves. As with the other exhortations in this book, the *inward* needs to precede the *outward.* It would be hypocritical, indeed, to have high expectations for others while not maintaining high personal standards. That is why the phrase "lead by example" has so much significance. That is why the Bible says anyone desiring to be a church leader (i.e. elder or deacon) should have his own house in order first (See 1 Timothy 3:1-13). "Do as I say, not as I do," is no way to live.

Yes, as long as we have high expectations for ourselves,

it is right and proper to have high expectations for others. In fact, it shows care and concern to do so. Who wants a coach that doesn't try to take individuals and teams to new heights? Who wants a teacher that never challenges students to think in new ways? Who wants a supervisor that doesn't try to help employees be more effective or productive? I would hypothesize that people who recoil from high expectations are fixed mindset people who just want to be left alone.

My Big Rocks are faith, family, and work; I have high expectations in these areas. I have high expectations for church leaders. Pastors need to share Bible-based messages that are well constructed and applicable to the lives of those listening. Elders, deacons, and Sunday school teachers need to be upright people who set a good example of Christian love and service. Spouses need to be faithful to each other and supportive of each other. They need to hold each other accountable, too, not enabling sinful human nature to run rampant. Parents need to be loving and understanding, but they need to be parents first. They need to discipline their children, understanding that the root word of *discipline* is *disciple*. They need to disciple, or teach, their children how to live. Employees need to set a good example at work. Working hard, being on time, and treating people right should be constants. Anyone in a position of responsibility should consistently exhibit these traits.

Doesn't everybody like to enjoy success, "the fruits of their labors"? Doesn't everyone thirst for a sense of accomplishment in life? High expectations for others and ourselves provide the avenue for accomplishing these things. Ralph Waldo Emerson once said, 'Nothing great was ever accomplished without enthusiasm." I agree, and

I think the same can be said of high expectations. As a coach, I always felt that players tended to rise to the level of expectations. Helping people realize their potential is what coaching is all about.

Don't be hesitant about having high expectations for yourself and others. I'm willing to bet that the teachers, coaches, and bosses you have appreciated most throughout your life saw potential in you and pushed you to develop that potential. They had high expectations. I understand that "we're only human," but I don't think we should meekly accept our baser nature. God has big plans for us, and they are only going to come to fruition if we have high expectations.

Chapter 3
"Love Your Neighbor"

"Even the disciples, who at times could be dense as bricks, realized that the true neighbor was the one who showed mercy to a stranger."

—Scott Russell Sanders

Robert Frost's excellent poem "Mending Wall" features a man who repeats, "Good fences make good neighbors," like a magical incantation. He likes the wall between his neighbor and him; he doesn't want anyone to get too close. A lot of people live like that, never letting down their guard. In fact, many people aren't just inwardly focused; they are actively building barriers against others. I can understand this tendency. There is vulnerability in just being real with other people.

Jesus' "two greatest commandments" give us a glimpse of how God intends us to live, and it is not with a "good fences make good neighbors" mentality. Jesus says the greatest commandment is to "love the Lord your God with all your heart, soul, mind, and strength," and the second is to "love your neighbor as yourself" (Matthew 22:38-39). And there you have it, the *upward* leads to the *outward.* If we are loving God with all our heart, soul, mind, and strength, we can't help but love our neighbor. Loving God enables us to see others through His eyes. He sees each person as the beautiful, unique individual He created in His own image. When we love our neighbor, we show our love for God.

Jesus communicated this beautifully to Peter, the Rock on which the Church is built (Matthew 16:18). Jesus asked Peter if he loved Him, and Peter replied, "You know I do, Lord." That is the *upward.* "Then feed my sheep," Jesus replied (John 21:15-16). That is the *outward.* The *upward* leads to the *outward.* The greatest commandment leads to the one like it.

In trying to help His followers understand the price of discipleship, Jesus told them they would have to pick up their cross and be ready to suffer. They were to make their lives living sacrifices as He did. He demonstrated love for them when He washed their feet. He demonstrated love for us when He hung on the cross. In the words of Christ, "No greater love is there than this: to lay down one's life for one's friends" (John 15:13).

Most of us probably love our friends. Even the pagans do, Jesus says (Matthew 5:47). Loving our neighbor kicks it up a notch. We have the same question the disciples did: "Just who is our neighbor?" Jesus says that whatever we do (or don't do) to the "least of these" we do (or don't do) to Him (Matthew 25:40-45). When you extend a helping hand to someone who is hurting, you are helping your neighbor. You are also showing your love to Christ. The Spirit moving in your life, the *inward*, causes you to behave in a Christ-like manner toward others, the *outward*, to the glory of God, the *upward*.

I love the beauty of the Trinity—the Father, Son, and Holy Spirit. God's design is flawless. His plan for the world and each one of us is perfect. The *inward*, *outward*, and *upward* exist in harmony as co-equals, like the three persons of the Trinity.

Love your neighbor (*outward*). In doing so, you love yourself (*inward*) and show your love for God (*upward*).

Chapter 4
"Walk the Talk"

"You can say you love someone – but unless you demonstrate that love through your actions, your words become meaningless."

—Stephen Covey

It is easy to be cynical these days when politicians routinely lie to the public and practice self-interest with no thought given to the well being of the people they represent. Of course, there are politicians who serve honorably and behave honestly (I want to believe so anyway). Politicians are by no means the only people who are hypocritical or disingenuous. People who put themselves forward as moral authorities have been caught in deviant sexual behaviors. World-class athletes have been exposed as users of performance enhancing drugs. Parents have prostituted their own children. These high profile examples are easy to point to, but all of us have wanted to portray a sparkling exterior when our heart was rotten and corroded on the inside at some time. How can I make a statement like that? Because I believe what Romans 3:23 says is true: "For all sin and fall short of the glory of God" (NIV).

If we really want to walk the talk, we have to start by acknowledging our imperfections. We have to be honest that we struggle with sin. I understand the desire to want to categorize sin by degree. Our society is all about measuring and comparing. Surely the sweet old lady who indulges in a little gossip or the honor student who engages in premarital sex aren't sinners of the magnitude of a murderer or rapist, are they? It's not that simple. Our God is a righteous God who cannot tolerate sin of any kind. 1 John 5:17 says all wrongdoing is sin, but it does seem to differentiate, saying not all sin leads to death. Fortunately we don't have to try to figure it out, and it is not our place to judge. In fact, we escape the judgment that sin brings when we accept Christ as our Savior because He has already paid the price of our sin. Once we feel the joy of this grace and let the Spirit move in our lives, we can begin to walk the talk.

Knowing the Bible and being able to articulate God's plan for our salvation equips us for the talk. Living as a disciple and striving to become more Christ-like is the walk. The more we let the Spirit guide us, the more discerning we become about God's Will for our lives. The more discerning we are, the more authentic our walk can become.

We can't discount the importance of our heart in this process. Motivation matters. King David was an adulterer and a murderer, but he was described as "a man after God's own heart" (Acts 13:22). He sinned but he admitted his sin and changed. He sinned big, but he also loved God big. If we love God as David did and have joy in our hearts for the grace we have been shown, then we will want to walk the talk. That is the power of motivation. Anyone who has been a parent, teacher, or coach understands how critical motivation is.

If we possess understanding, thankfulness, and motivation, walking the talk becomes less of an unnatural effort or burden and more of a labor of love. In time we may become the kind of saints who seem to walk the talk naturally, suffused with the Spirit. I bet we have all known people like that.

Chapter 5
"Enjoy People"

"I love mankind. . .it's people I can't stand!"
—Charles Schultz

Probably most of us have had a moment when we felt what Charles Schultz expressed above. Life is so much more satisfying if we can learn to enjoy people, though. As I have gotten older and have learned to enjoy people more, I have gotten better at appreciating people's individuality and their strengths. I have gotten more forgiving about their faults. This progress in the *outward* realm would not have been possible until the *inward* was in order. For me, it was similar to the Biblical instruction that one who wants to be a church leader needs to have his own house in order first (1 Timothy 3:4). Until I could like myself, I couldn't relax and like other people. This self-loathing had nothing to do with talents or accomplishments; it had everything to do with the kind of person I was. Once I fully appreciated the power and necessity of God's grace, I was able to have a repentant heart and start living for God. As I did that, I was much more able to accept each person I met as one of God's precious children. Then it became much easier to enjoy people. You probably see the *upward* creeping in here: seeing people through God's eyes. That really is the whole point of this book—connecting *inward, outward,* and *upward* so that we can live the kind of fruitful and joyous life God intends for us.

On the everyday, practical level life is just so much more satisfying if we can enjoy people. I believe humans are created to be social. Most people have a number of human interactions every day: from the gas station, grocery store, or restaurant to the office, church, or social gathering to the quiet night at home, sports event, or family vacation. We impact others every time we cross paths with other people. We enjoy it when someone smiles at us, thanks us, holds a door for us, or says he/she enjoyed meeting us. Why wouldn't we want to leave every person we meet with a positive afterglow? Aren't we supposed to be salt and light in the world (Matthew 5:13-16)? Don't we want to leave the world a better place due to our existence? Don't we want to add value to any group we are a part of? I think we should. An important part of that is enjoying people so that we can share positive energy and optimism.

I understand people have different personalities, and not everyone is naturally social. My wife and I have had interesting conversations about this topic. Whether you are an introvert, extrovert, or somewhere in between, I really believe you can learn to appreciate and enjoy people. Once you can do that, the next hurdle becomes being able to express that appreciation. There is power in letting others know you enjoy and appreciate them. I often use the written word to do that, but the spoken word is very powerful as well. Perhaps more important to remember is the old adage, "Actions speak louder than words." We brand ourselves hypocrites if we tell people we enjoy and appreciate them but our actions don't match our words. Living in a state of appreciation requires getting beyond our own gratification to a mindset where we want to serve and make others' lives better. Enjoying people is important. Helping others enjoy people can have a great positive impact in a "pay it forward" kind of way.

Jesus enjoyed people. He broke bread with His disciples and invested in their development. He prepared them to spread the Good News and receive His kingdom. Many times in the Bible he was moved with compassion to help and heal others. He allowed His inner circle glimpses of the divine at His baptism and transfiguration. His vulnerability and power were both on public display with His crucifixion and resurrection. The God of the Universe came to Earth as a man who made time for children, ate dinner with the despised, and wept at the suffering of others. Jesus enjoyed people and cared about them deeply. Shouldn't we?

Chapter 6
"In Your Relationships with Others, Who are You?"

"Love sought is good, but given unsought, is better."
—William Shakespeare

"In your relationships with others, who are you?" This is an extremely challenging question. To answer thoughtfully and accurately requires self-knowledge first. Before we can assess our relationships with others, we need to be honest about our motivations and our biases. Answering this question adequately requires discernment. Relationships, by definition, involve others, and we have to be able to accurately assess our impact on others and gauge their feelings toward us before we can answer who we are in our relationships with others. Truly, only others can answer this question for us, and if we do not communicate, we will never know. I wonder how people would respond, once they got past their initial shock and incredulity, if we genuinely asked them, "Am I loving you like I love myself?" How are we doing with the second "great commandment" to love our neighbors as ourselves that I wrote about several chapters ago (Matthew 22:38-39)? Do we extend the kind of love and patience we appreciate from others? Do we reflect God's unconditional love for us in our daily dealings with others? The *inward, outward,* and *upward* converge with these important questions. Self-knowledge demonstrates the inward. Impact on others speaks to the outward. God's Will for our lives addresses the upward. All of these elements play out in our lives and are on display for the world. "All the world's a stage and all the men and women merely players," Shakespeare wrote *(As You Like It*, Act II, Scene VII). What does the drama of our lives say about our commitment to live in love with others?

Knowing ourselves and loving ourselves begins with being honest with ourselves. The tax collector's prayer in Luke 18 gets right to the heart of the matter: "God have mercy on me, a sinner." We need to get beyond all of our pride, vanity, and ambition so that we can admit we are flawed and imperfect. If we can do that, then we will become more understanding of and accepting of others' imperfections and less likely to "look at the speck of sawdust in our brother's eye and ignore the plank in our own" (Matthew 7:3). We need to be able to enter into relationship with others on equal footing, recognizing that both parties are beloved children of God (1 John 3:2) just as both parties are flawed sinners (Romans 3:23). The Bible actually implores us to humble ourselves and think of ourselves as lower than others.

The Apostle Paul considered himself "chief among sinners" (1 Timothy 1:15), and Jesus noted that the physician comes to heal the sick (Mark 2:17). Jesus advised His followers with an example they could understand: "When someone invites you to a wedding feast, do not take the place of honor, for a person more distinguished than you may have been invited. If so, the host who invited both of you will come and say to you, 'Give this person your seat.' Then, humiliated, you will have to take the least important place. But when you are invited, take the lowest place, so that when your host comes, he will say to you, 'Friend, move up to a better place.' Then you will be honored in the presence of all the other guests" (Luke 14:8-10). "For those who exalt themselves will be humbled, and those who humble themselves will be exalted," Matthew 23:12 states quite clearly. Although our society provides plenty of example of self-aggrandizement and people who seem to be succeeding in their arrogance, this is not God's model and it is not how we are called to be in relationship with others. People appreciate true humility, and if we are really honest with ourselves, it should not be that hard to be humble.

Jesus Christ humbled Himself to the point of death on a cross. Although people were amazed by His miracles and the authority of His teaching, He responded to others with service and compassion. He washed His disciples' feet. He healed the masses. He also pushed people to be their best and live in accordance with God's Will. The extent to which we can imitate the Master will determine the answer to that question, "In your relationships with others, who are you?"

Section 3 — Upward

Chapter 1
"Be Real With God"

"God has given you one face, and you make yourself another."
—William Shakespeare

Being real with God is really kind of a non sequitur if you believe in an omniscient God. The Bible tells us God "knit me together in my mother's womb," (Psalm 139:13), "knows the plans He has for us," (Jeremiah 29:11), and knows the number of hairs on our heads (Luke 12:7). Do you really think we can fool God? I know we try to, and we try to bargain with Him, but really this *upward* problem begins with the *inward* problem of not being honest with ourselves or the *outward* problem of not loving others as we are called to.

If you have been a parent, you have some understanding of the challenge of being real with God. Even great kids will try to manipulate their parents to try to get what they want. Children are egocentric. They want what they want, and they generally want to stay out of trouble. Through the years I have resisted laughing out loud when parents have said, "I know my kid. My kid wouldn't lie to me." Newsflash: kids lie. So do adults. That's why, "Do not bear false witness," made God's top ten.

Drop the pretenses. God knows your most petty, selfish, or perverted thought. Thank goodness we don't know everything our kids have thought, said, and done, and thank goodness our parents didn't know everything we thought, said, and did! I am flashing back to the Lutheran Order of Confession and Forgiveness: "We have not loved You with our whole heart. We have not loved our neighbors as ourselves. We have sinned against You in thought, word, and deed, by what we have done and what we have left undone." Yeah, that just about covers it. Fortunately, our God is big enough to handle all of this sin, and He sent His Son to redeem us! On Judgment Day all pretense will be stripped away; it will be our God and us. It will be real. I have a feeling that if we can learn to be real with God now, we will be able to more confidently approach His throne then.

I have always liked the courtroom drama, and here's one that speaks directly to this topic. It is shared online under the title "Judgment," and I found it at www.frtommylane.com :

After living a "decent" life, my time on earth came to an end. The first thing I remember is sitting on a bench in the waiting room of what I thought to be a courthouse. The doors opened and I was instructed to come in and have a seat by the defense table. As I looked around, I saw the "prosecutor": he was a villainous looking gent who snarled as he stared at me. He definitely was the most evil person

I have ever seen. I sat down and looked to my left, and there sat my lawyer, a kind and gentle looking man whose appearance seemed very familiar to me.

The corner door flew open and there appeared the judge in full flowing robes. He commanded an awesome presence as he moved across the room, and I couldn't take my eyes off of him. As he took his seat behind the bench he said, "Let us begin."

The prosecutor rose and said, "My name is Satan and I am here to show you why this man belongs in Hell." He proceeded to tell of lies that I told, things that I stole and in the past when I cheated others. Satan told of other horrible perversions that were once in my life and the more he spoke, the further down in my seat I sank. I was so embarrassed that I couldn't look at anyone, even my own lawyer, as the Devil told of sins that even I had completely forgotten about.

As upset as I was at Satan for telling all these things about me, I was equally upset at my representative, who sat there silently, not offering any form of defense at all. I know I had been guilty of those things, but I had done some good in my life – couldn't that at least equal out part of the harm I've done?

Satan finished with a fury and said, "This man belongs in Hell, he is guilty of all that I have charged and there is not a person who can prove otherwise!"

When it was his turn, my lawyer first asked if he might approach the bench. The judge allowed this, over the strong objection of Satan, and beckoned him to come forward. As he got up and started walking, I was able to see him now in his full splendor and majesty. Now I realized why he seemed so familiar. This was Jesus representing me, my

Lord and my Savior. He stopped at the bench and softly said to the judge, "Hi, Dad," and then he turned to address the court.

"Satan was correct in saying that this man had sinned; I won't deny any of these allegations. And yes, the wage of sins is death and this man deserves to be punished." Jesus took a deep breath and turned to his Father with outstretched arms and proclaimed, "However, I died on the cross so that this person might have eternal life and he has accepted me as his Savior, so he is mine."

My Lord continued with, "His name is written in the Book of Life and no one can snatch him from me. Satan still does not understand yet, this man is not to be given justice, but rather mercy." As Jesus sat down, he quietly paused, looked at his Father and replied, "There is nothing else that needs to be done. I've done it all."

The Judge lifted his mighty hand and slammed the gavel down and the following words bellowed from his lips: "This man is free - the penalty for him has already been paid in full, case dismissed."

As my Lord led me away I could hear Satan ranting and raving, "I won't give up. I'll win the next one!" I asked Jesus as he gave me my instructions on where to go next, "Have you ever lost a case?" Christ lovingly smiled and said, "Everyone that has come to me and asked me to represent them has received the same verdict as you...Paid in Full."

Be real with God. Those of you with older children, do you remember when your relationship with your kids began to feel more like a true friendship and less like you were lawgivers? I do. I remember reaching that point as a young adult, too. We serve an awesome God, one who created us and will judge us, but one who wants a personal relationship, too. That's why He came to earth as a human in the form of Christ, and that's why He sent the Spirit to work in our lives. Be real with God. You won't be sorry.

Chapter 2
"Seek to be Holy"

"There will be no great Revival until the people of God are deeply convicted of their need of holiness."

—Major Allistaire Smith, Salvation Army

The *upward* kicks it up a notch from, "Have high expectations," to "Seek to be holy." Picture this. Someone asks you, "What is your biggest goal right now?" and you reply, "I'm seeking to be holy." They might roll their eyes or give you a blank stare while trying to decide if you are a Jesus freak or a budding cult leader. The simple truth is that seeking to be holy is precisely what followers of Christ are called to do.

Believers are to be holy, or set apart. Hebrews 10:10 says, "We have been set apart as holy because Jesus Christ did what God wanted him to do by sacrificing his body once and for all" (God's Word Translation). We are in a position of being in this world but not of this world. Romans 12:2

counsels, "Do not conform to the pattern of this world, but be transformed by the renewing of your mind" (NIV). We exist to glorify God and to strive to become more Christ-like. Can we rise to the high expectations God has for us?

Is living for our Creator important enough that we can risk alienating other people? Some will think our quest for righteousness is self-righteousness. Some will think trying to be holy is acting "holier-than-thou." We do need to guard against becoming judgmental. We have to guard our hearts so that we don't become like the hypocritical Pharisees of Jesus' day. Some will see us as narrow-minded even if we are just trying following our beliefs because they are convicted by their own sinfulness.

People are quick to note that God is love and Jesus is tenderhearted, and that is true. Jesus is clear that people need to pick sides, though: "Do you think I have come to bring peace on earth? No, I tell you, but rather division" (Luke 12:51 ESV). He will divide the sheep and the goats (Matthew 25:31-33) and the wheat from the chaff (Matthew 3:12). I believe there is an often-misunderstood notion of tolerance today that says people shouldn't take a clear stand if others disagree with it. We are afraid of hurting others' feelings or of being viewed as extremists. These concerns melt away if we make the Bible our standard.

Our quest for righteousness now, today, will have eternal consequences. Motives matter with God, though, and seeking to be holy needs to flow from our love of God and His Spirit moving in our lives, not from a misguided effort to earn our salvation. Nothing we can do is good enough to earn us the label *holy*; but Christ, in fact, sanctifies us. Our attempts to become holy are a tribute to our Savior.

If you have confessed your sin and believe Jesus is the Son of God, you are saved. You will have eternity with God. Striving to be holy in this life will bring a measure of heaven on earth. Jesus said, "The Kingdom of God is already among you" (Luke 17:21). Living like that is true makes us salt and light for the world. Matthew 5:13-16 says, "Let me tell you why you are here. You're here to be salt-seasoning that brings out the God-flavors of this earth. If you lose your saltiness, how will people taste godliness? You've lost your usefulness and will end up in the garbage. Here's another way to put it: You're here to be light, bringing out the God-colors in the world. God is not a secret to be kept. We're going public with this, as public as a city on a hill. If I make you light-bearers, you don't think I'm going to hide you under a bucket, do you? I'm putting you on a light stand. Now that I've put you there on a hilltop, on a light stand—shine! Keep open house; be generous with your lives. By opening up to others, you'll prompt people to open up with God, this generous Father in heaven" (MSG). If we live like this, we are living up to the exhortation, "Seek to be holy."

Chapter 3
"Love as He Loves Us"

"The truth is that each of us fall short of loving unconditionally. We don't love others the way God loves us. Yet Jesus extended perfect love by living and dying for all of our sins. In spite of our failures, weaknesses, and selfishness, He sacrificed His own life so we could have eternal life."

—Dana Arcuri

Many people have probably heard, "We love because He first loved us" (1 John 4:19). I am sure that is true. Showing love is a learned behavior for the most part, excluding "maternal instinct," or the intrinsic need to nurture. People learn to love from their families and other significant people in their lives. People who do not have the blessing of loving parents often have a lifetime of learning how to love. I think of orphans in the former Soviet Union, for example. Many of these children were never held as babies. They received no human touch, and the result is often an attachment disorder that makes it very difficult for them to show or receive affection.

Even if we accept that we love because He first loved us, loving *as* He loves us provides an incredible challenge. Loving as God loves is often described as *unconditional love*. How do we, as humans, accomplish this? I think a good number of people love their spouses and children unconditionally, no matter what. It is a lot easier to love your kids when they're getting good grades, staying out of trouble, working hard, and being polite than when they are making bad decisions, worrying you sick, being disrespectful, or hanging out with a bad crowd, though, isn't it? It's a lot easier to love your spouse when he/she remembers your anniversary, pulls his/her weight around the house, is attractive and romantic, and agrees with us than when he/she finds fault, displays that annoying habit, questions our decisions, or gives us the cold shoulder. All of these things are factors that creep into our lives and make it a challenge to love unconditionally.

Let's back up a minute and try to wrap our brains around what it means to love as God loves. It is impossible to comprehend God's greatness and the depth of His love. The best we can do is to look at His actions. First of all, He created this beautiful, complex universe for us to enjoy and wonder at. God spoke the universe into existence and proclaimed that it was good. He didn't put it on a shelf to pick up and admire from time to time like a celestial snow globe. Instead, He created man and woman, you and me, to have dominion over it and enjoy it. Think about loving people enough to hand over your creation, your prized possession, to them for their enjoyment. Imagine lovingly restoring a vintage muscle car until it was perfect then tossing the keys to an irresponsible teenager and saying, "Enjoy." That's about what God did for us.

Of course, God's love didn't end once He created the Earth. Earth didn't stay pristine and perfect like the Garden of Eden was. When sin entered the world, suffering and death were close behind. The Roman poet Virgil might not have had God's love in mind when he wrote, "Amor vincit omnia," or "Love conquers all," to you and me. However, God's love does conquer all, including sin and death. Probably the first Bible verse many people ever see tells the story: "For God so loved the world, He gave His only begotten Son, that whosoever believeth in him should not perish, but have everlasting life" (John 3:16, KJV).

Now we're really getting at the heart of what it means to love as God loves, loving sacrificially. Jesus spoke repeatedly to His disciples about this. He lived sacrificial love first, and He counted the cost of discipleship for His followers. He told them, "Greater love has no one than this: to lay down one's life for one's friends." (John 15:13, NIV). He told them they needed to pick up their cross and follow him (Matthew 16:24). He said once they committed, they needed to keep their hand on the plow (Luke 9:62). He called them his friends (John 15:15). He said whoever did the will of God was His family (Mark 3:35).

Would you really aspire to love as God loves? We are called to do that as Christians. We are called to make our lives "living sacrifices" (Romans 12:1). We are told to love our neighbors (Mark 12:31). We are told to forgive over and over again (Matthew 18:22). All of these actions run counter to our selfish human nature. We instinctively seek comfort, not sacrifice. We want to get even, not forgive. We are called to be better, though. We are children of the

Living God! We should spend our lives striving to be more loving and more lovable.

I admire the example of Mother Teresa, or Teresa of Calcutta. She sacrificially loved the poorest, most pathetic, disease-ridden people on earth in the slums of Calcutta, India. She embodied Jesus' direction, "That which you do to the least of these, you do to me" (Matthew 25:40).

Mother Teresa's name recognition is very high. Her good deeds are well known. Less well known is the fact that she suffered from long, severe bouts of depression. Writings she left behind tell of crises of faith she suffered. However, her love for others was constant. She practiced what she preached in her "Anyway" poem. That poem reminds us that sacrificial love, as the term implies, is never easy:

> People are often unreasonable, illogical and
> self-centered;
> Forgive them anyway.
>
> If you are kind, people may accuse you of selfish,
> ulterior motives;
> Be kind anyway.
>
> If you are successful, you will win some false friends
> and some true enemies;
> Succeed anyway.
>
> If you are honest and frank, people may cheat you;
> Be honest and frank anyway.
>
> What you spend years building, someone could
> destroy overnight;
> Build anyway.

If you find serenity and happiness, they may be jealous;
Be happy anyway.

The good you do today, people will often forget tomorrow;
Do good anyway.

Give the world the best you have, and it may never be enough;
Give the world the best you've got anyway.

You see, in the final analysis, it is between you and your God;
It was never between you and them anyway.

Here's a lifetime challenge that you will never master: love as God loves. Think of the impact you can have by just trying, though. Mother Teresa is a good example; there are many others, such as Albert Schweitzer, Harriet Tubman, the Apostle Paul, or the ultimate example, Jesus Christ.

In his letter to the Galatians, Paul provided a couple of great reminders and attitude checks. He wrote, "If you think you are too important to help someone, you are only fooling yourself. You are not that important" (Galatians 6:3, NLT). We aren't important. It's not about us. "What is important," Paul wrote, "is faith expressing itself in love" (Galatians 5:6, NLT).

Every journey begins with a single step. What can you do today to be more loving?

Chapter 4
"Be a Living Sacrifice"

"Therefore, I urge you, brothers and sisters, in view of God's mercy, to offer your bodies as a living sacrifice, holy and pleasing to God—this is your true and proper worship. Do not conform to the pattern of this world, but be transformed by the renewing of your mind. Then you will be able to test and approve what God's will is—his good, pleasing and perfect will."

—Romans 12:1-2 (NIV)

Without fail, when I read the parts of the Old Testament that detail different kinds of sacrifices and offerings, I get bogged down. I have to remind myself, "All Scripture is God-breathed and is useful for teaching, rebuking, correcting and training in righteousness" (2 Timothy 3:16, NIV). As I have studied the Bible through the years, I have come to appreciate the role of the Law and the Old Testament covenant, however. It was inevitable that sinful human nature would condemn people under the Law, in spite of leaders God raised up and miraculous intervention. The Law, with its accompanying sacrifices, was merely a placeholder, a stop-gap, until God's redemptive plan and the New Covenant of Christ's blood could be enacted.

Understanding that "the wages of sin is death" (Romans 6:23, KJV) and that nothing we can do, no right living, can earn us salvation is necessary to appreciate grace. The Jewish religious leaders of Jesus' time could not get to this point. They were caught up in their self-righteousness and a continual cycle of man-made ritual. They were zealous, and no one was more zealous than Saul. Saul enthusiastically persecuted early Christians until his well-known Damascus Road conversion (See Acts 9).

Saul became Paul, and the recognition of his previous sin helped him understand and appreciate grace fully. When Paul exhorts people to make their lives living sacrifices, he does so with an understanding of what this entails. Many times he was "in chains for Christ" (Philippians 1:13, NIV). He learned "to be content whatever the circumstances" (Philippians 4:11, NIV), reporting, "Three times I was beaten with rods, once I was pelted with stones, three times I was shipwrecked, I spent a night and a day in the open sea" (2 Corinthians 11:25, NIV). Paul's transformation from persecutor of Christ to apostle to the Gentiles and author of a large portion of the Bible was remarkable. He poured his life out as a living sacrifice.

Most responsible adults understand sacrifice. Even though our society does not encourage delaying gratification for a moment, many people are willing to sacrifice now for something greater later. Parents teach their children that hard work pays off. Employees put in extra time at work to ensure a project's success. Spouses put aside their personal preferences for those of their husbands and wives. Some people give sacrificially of their time, resources, and selves and not just out of their abundance.

All of these actions can be admirable, and they might be outward manifestations of being a living sacrifice, but as I wrote in "Walk the Talk," motivation matters. God doesn't need our money. He wants our heart. If our hearts are right, good deeds will follow. As the well known song says, "And they'll know we are Christians by our love."

If we hope to make our lives living sacrifices, we have to surrender our lives to God. We cannot compartmentalize, relegating God to Sunday and living our daily lives independent of Him. Even if we are "good people," God wants more. He wants all of us.

Being a living sacrifice is not easy, and it is not something to be considered flippantly. Even Christ, God made flesh, struggled. Jesus was tempted by the same things we are: physical needs and comforts, power, and fame (See Matthew 4). He struggled to fulfill God's plan for His life and prayed for another way (See Matthew 26). In the end He willingly gave His life and was honored by a seat at the right hand of God (Luke 22:69). He tried to help His disciples understand that He came to serve (Matthew 20:28, Mark 10:45, John 13:1-17). He clearly told them that there was a cost to discipleship, and they would suffer if they chose to follow Him (Luke 14:25-33). The same is true for you and me.

Are you ready and willing to turn your life over to God? To do so means you will be a slave to Christ. Before you bristle at that idea, puffing out your chest and saying, "I'm no one's slave!" consider Romans 6:18, which says that once we are freed as slaves from sin, we become slaves to righteousness. Would you rather be a willing, enthusiastic slave to Christ or a doomed, ignorant slave to sin?

Begin with a willingness to follow Jesus, wherever He might lead you. Study the Bible. Worship. Abide in prayer. Open yourself to the Spirit and let God use you. As you have a daily walk with the Creator, you will find your life becoming more and more a living sacrifice.

Chapter 5
"Be Who God Intends You to Be"

"Every human being is intended to have a character of his own; to be what no others are, and to do what no other can do."

—William Ellery Channing

I would hazard a guess that many people spend much of their lives trying to figure out who they are and what they should be doing. This search for identity is not limited to the child who is first testing boundaries or the adolescent who is making life-altering decisions in a hormone-clouded haze. The mid-life crisis or "dark night of the soul" (See St. John of the Cross's poem) might come along after one would think a person has life all figured out. Why does life have to be so difficult? Wouldn't it be a lot easier to be handed an itinerary to follow? I know when I was a classroom teacher I heard, "Just tell me what you want me to do," from plenty of students when I took a constructivist approach and expected them to think for themselves and construct their own meaning.

Many people try to make life formulaic. Parents do this for their kids, trying to predetermine what their future should be, grooming them for greatness. Goal-oriented people do this for themselves, creating signposts years out to judge adequate progress toward the end they want for themselves. Of course, as Robert Burns and John Steinbeck illustrated so well, "The best-laid plans of mice and men often go awry, leaving nothing but grief and pain for promised joy" (See Burns's poem "To a Mouse" and Steinbeck's novel *Of Mice and Men*).

Rick Warren wrote convincingly about finding one's purpose in *The Purpose-Driven Life*, a book I enjoyed and have recommended. Warren's book pushes the reader to be introspective and to think about the kind of life God wants for him/her. This way of thinking is really important for people in a society that is so focused on visible manifestations and is so results-based. I am convinced that God cares much more about <u>who</u> I am than about <u>what</u> I am, in terms of career, political persuasion, civic affiliations, or any other labels society might be concerned with.

Another author I have benefited from reading is Stephen Covey. One of his *7 Habits of Highly Effective People* is, "Put first things first." The Bible says, "But seek ye first the kingdom of God, and his righteousness; and all these things shall be added unto you" (Matthew 6:23, KJV). I interpret "all these things" to be the blessings that are by-products of being who God intends you to be. He <u>wants</u> to bless us. The more attuned we become to His will for our lives, the happier and more productive we are, and the more opportunities we will have to share His love with others. Several verses in the Bible promise that people who have blessings will be given even more (Matthew 13:12, Matthew 25:29, Mark 4:25, Luke 8:18); this is the abundance God wants to give to people who seek Him. Luke 12:48 also reminds us, "Everyone to whom much was given, of him much will be required" (NIV). I don't think we need to shy away from that. High expectations are a good thing, an invigorating thing, especially when we know we do not have to rely solely on ourselves.

God equips us to grow into the kind of people He wants us to be, and it is a process, a daily walk. I think one of the cleanest, most beautiful explanations of what God wants of us occurs in Micah 6:8: "He has shown you, O mortal, what is good. And what does the Lord require of you? To act justly and to love mercy and to walk humbly with your God" (NIV). *The Message* translation says it even more clearly and conversationally: "But he's already made it plain how to live, what to do, what God is looking for in men and women. It's quite simple: Do what is fair and just to your neighbor, be compassionate and loyal in your love, And don't take yourself too seriously—take God seriously."

Would our lives be enriched if we consistently did these things? Would our world be a different place if people everywhere were focused on being fair, just, loyal, and compassionate? Before you dismiss this as an impossibility, I encourage you to start with yourself, with what you can control. Mahatma Gandhi gave some good advice when he said, "Be the change you wish to see in the world." My prayer for you and for me is that every day we can strive to be who God intends us to be.

Chapter 6
"Are You Right with God?"

"Even if you have got nothing else left, be proud of your relationship with God."

—Sunday Adelaja

God is a relational being. The term *Godhead* is used to denote Father, Son, and Holy Spirit: three interrelated, equal, and distinct persons. It occurs to me that *inward*, *outward*, and *upward* are reflected in their persons. The Spirit is an inward manifestation. It is the wise counselor sent to guide us the way the Father would have us go. Jesus Christ is the outward, visible manifestation of God's love. God incarnate, or *made flesh*, is who Jesus is. He is God's emissary to a world full of His wayward children. God the Father is whom we cast our eyes upon, upward in Heaven. Because He created us in His image, we have a spark of the divine in us, we have souls, and we long to be reunited with Him. When we are right with God, we recognize His relational nature and understand that He seeks to draw us near to Him.

How do we go about having a personal relationship with our creator? I believe we need to be seekers. We have to long to enter into His presence. The psalmist, David, prayed and wrote and sang praises to God. He cried out in anguish when he was beset by enemies and when he lost his son. God heard him and called David a man after His own heart (Acts 13:22).

Moses spoke with God face-to-face (Exodus 33:11). His face was so radiant when he came down off the mountain that he had to wear a veil in the presence of others (Exodus 34:29-35). Moses had his shortcomings. Like David, he was responsible for ending a life. He made excuses when God called him to lead, and he was prevented from entering the Promised Land; but he was right with God.

Job was sorely tested. He suffered and lost his worldly wealth and children. His wife told him to curse God and die (Job 2:9). He did not do that, but he did question God. In the end he remained true, and he acknowledged God's sovereignty. Job was right with God.

There are many more Biblical examples of people right with God. Noah was the only blameless person living on earth (Genesis 6:9), and Abraham's faith was credited as righteousness (Genesis 15:6). Jesus Christ is obviously right with God. He is God, but He is fully human, too, and He overcame temptations and suffering to fulfill God's plan perfectly and announce, "It is finished," from the cross (John 19:30). Stephen, the Church's first martyr, was right with God, too. When he was stoned to death, he implored God in the same way Jesus did from the cross, "Lord, do not hold this sin against them" (Acts 7:60, NIV).

You may not be called upon to give your life to be right with God, but you are directed to make your life a "living sacrifice" (Romans 12:1). If you are able to die to this world, then you can live in Christ. This is what it is to be born again, but some people today understand the concept no better than Nicodemus did when he went to visit Jesus one night (John 3).

Are you right with God? Do you "hunger and thirst for righteousness" (Matthew 5:6)? Does your soul long for God like the deer pants for the water (Psalm 42:1)? You can confess your sins, be baptized, attend church regularly, give generously, read the Bible, and pray. All of these are outward signs of being a believer. The Bible says, "Only God knows the human heart" (Romans 2:2, NIV). Only God and you know if you are right with God. If you have any doubts, I urge you to seek a closer walk with Him. If you <u>are</u> right with God, you are already seeking one.

My prayer for you is that you are so much in the grip of grace, so overwhelmed with God's love for you, that you can't help but share your faith and His love with others. Regardless of your age, gender, ethnicity, career, or any other measure you can think of, I pray that you are right with God and that He has you right where He wants you, in relationship with Him.

Afterword

As an English teacher and teacher of writing, I always encouraged students to carefully consider audience and purpose as they wrote. My parting words to you do just that. Let me start with purpose: my purpose in writing is to put into words the overwhelming thankfulness I have for the life and opportunities I have been given. I have been richly blessed in faith, family, and work. I am so thankful for God's love and grace, my incredible family, and all of the truly outstanding people I have been blessed to meet and work with. I also hope that this book can help the reader gain some clarity about his/her own beliefs and offer encouragement to people who might be struggling. This book will not make me a wealthy, best-selling author. It could potentially help someone somewhere, though, and that would be great. My audience might be small and might consist mainly of people who know me. I don't care so much about who reads the book; I just hope that someone who will benefit from it sees the title, picks it up, and comes to have a clearer picture of his/her own values (inward), stronger relationships with others (outward), and a new appreciation of the love God shows us (upward).

Other Books by Art Sathoff

40 Days to Reflection and Peace: Thoughts for Busy People and Ethical Leaders

Another 40 Days of Faith, Family, Work, and Fun

www.ingramcontent.com/pod-product-compliance
Lightning Source LLC
LaVergne TN
LVHW091205080426
835509LV00006B/836

* 9 7 8 1 4 2 1 8 3 7 4 7 5 *